BUILDING A LIFE AND CAREER IN SECURITY

A GUIDE FROM DAY 1 TO BUILDING A LIFE AND CAREER IN INFORMATION SECURITY

JAY SCHULMAN

Continue to Get Information On Growing Your Information Security Career at:

JaySchulman.com

Building A Life and Career in Security

Print Edition:

ISBN 978-0-69251-415-3

Why I Wrote This Book

From college to today, my career has taken an atypical road. I did not wake up in High School and say, "I want to be in information security." In fact, I thought I should stay away from technology altogether because it was too fun to make into a career.

While I have had great mentors throughout the years, I have agonized over many decisions and, in hindsight, made some goofy choices. Overall, I have been very lucky.

Some of that luck created lessons that are teachable. As I have looked at my own path and helped others along their journey, I believe there is a framework for success in information security.

My goal in writing this book is to give you the confidence to grow your own career in information security. I have analyzed my career and the careers of others to design a plan to build a successful career in information security.

Nothing in this book is going to teach you the content. Instead, my focus is on how you can use the content you know and expand your knowledge base to give you an advantage in getting a promotion or moving to a new opportunity.

In the short term, this book can be your mentor to guiding your career. As you will read in the chapters ahead, I encourage you to get your own mentor to help you on a day-to-day basis with the unique problems you may face. (Make sure they have read the book too!)

Thanks for reading the book and I hope you find it valuable.

How You Should Use This Book

The book is a more in-depth guide to what I write about at JaySchulman.com. I have put together a set of bonuses including videos and supplementary materials for readers of the book. To get the bonuses, go to JaySchulman.com/book-bonus and download them now.

The book itself is split up into three sections, Day 1, Year 1 and Year 10. Before you jump right to where you are in your career, I would encourage you to read the book straight through. I think this is especially true if you are going to mentor someone in security.

Day 1

Day 1 is for people just starting their career in information security. It is great for people thinking about information security as a career or just about to start a job in the field. If you have been in security longer than a year, I encourage you to read this chapter so you can better help others you work with or learn how to mentor to help someone who looks up to you grow their career. It is foundational to the rest of the book..

Year 1

Year 1 is designed to build the skills to move from a doer to a manager. It might seem early to start thinking about management, but these skills are not learned overnight. I could also call this section, "How To Be A Great Manager," so even if you are already to this stage in your career, there are great tips to improving your own security management skills.

YEAR 10

Year 10 is about moving from a manager or director to a Security Executive. At this stage, it is less about the technical knowledge and more about how you deliver and communicate security messages to your stakeholders. Even if you are just getting into security today, it is important to understand the role of a Chief Information Security Officer. While the section will help you drive your career long-term, it will also help you better communicate the needs of the top security professional.

TABLE OF CONTENTS

Other Books By Jay Schulman

One Last Thing...

CHAPTER 1. DAY 1

Welcome. Over the next chapter, I will walk through the foundation of starting a career in information security. Even if you have been in the field for a while, you will find a lot of information you can use today. If you are a mentor to an aspiring or junior information security professional, this chapter will help you guide them in their career journey.

GETTING STARTED

There are many paths into an information security career. Personally, I started off as a network engineer focused on routers and switches. Configuring routers led to configuring firewalls which led to protecting servers and devices on the network. All of the sudden, security was a lot more fun than standard network engineering. Below, I will walk through a number of different paths into the security field. Your specific path probably fits into one of the generic paths below. There are so many different paths into security, it's hard to include them all. One of these three should still relate to you.

STRAIGHT OUT OF SCHOOL

This is relatively new. A number of schools are teaching information security or allowing students to focus on security as part of a larger computer science or technology program.

I do not focus on degrees. I do not think a specific degree gives you a leg up on anyone else. I have seen great security professionals who hold degrees in Computer Science, Electrical Engineering, and even English.

If you are in school today and know that you would like to focus on information security as a career, here is the best advice I can give you:

Get as broad of a technology education as possible. Once you find something that you love, we have a tendency to want to take as many classes in it as we can. Security is an overlay across all of technology. The more you understand technology, the better you can apply security to it.

Specifically, I would make sure to take classes in application development, networks, architecture, systems, and risk management. I would also try to take some business management courses to broaden your horizon as well.

The best security people are able to understand the technology and business components and appropriately mitigate risk.

THE NETWORK ROUTE

If you do not get into security as your first job, this is the most common route. Historically, security was a natural extension of the skillsets needed to be a network engineer. To manage a firewall, you need to understand IP Addressing, Ports, Protocols and overall networking.

Many of the security tools, such as NMAP and Nessus, assume a basic understanding of how networks work.

Given a network background, you have a high likelihood of success in security. I would challenge you to not rely upon the network to secure your environment. Pieces of infrastructure (such as firewalls, intrusion detection systems, web application firewalls) can only do so much to protect your applications and users.

As you enter a career in security, begin to learn about all of the non-network components that make up a good security program.

THE DEVELOPER ROUTE

Developers and anyone in the development area are sorely needed in information security. It makes sense that development organizations don't always get along with security organizations. It's a bunch of network people telling a bunch of development people how to code.

The best route for a developer to join a security organization is to focus on application security. As your first task, head over to OWASP (https://schl.mn/bacis01) and check out their resources; especially the OWASP Top 10 here (http://schl.mn/bacis02). The ten most common security bugs found in web applications.

While a developer can take any route once in a security organization, I think you can make the most significant impact on application security.

CORE KNOWLEDGE

There is foundational knowledge I think every information security person should have. No matter what part of information security you focus on, you should know these things. Quick warning: As you go through this, you might roll your eyes and say, "everyone knows this." They do not. Everyone comes into security with a different background. While most know some of the items in this list, some are definitely missing pieces.

Ports and IP Addressing

While this is very network centric, it is important in all aspects of security. You should understand what a port is and how protocols work. Additionally, you should know some common ports and what typically runs on them. For a quick primer checkout:

Understanding TCP Ports and Protocols here (http://schl.mn/bacis03)

List of TCP and UDP Ports here (http://schl.mn/bacis04)

Additionally, understanding IP Addressing is really important as well. There are two key components everyone should understanding: How to Subnet and Private IP Addresses. To learn about each of those, go to:

How to Subnet here (http://schl.mn/bacis05)

Private IP Addresses here (http://schl.mn/bacis06)

The OSI Model

The OSI Model or Open Systems Interconnection Model outlines how interconnected systems communicate. It is also referred to as the 7 Layer Model (because there are 7 layers!). No doubt in some meeting, you'll hear someone trying to sound smart and say, "that's just a layer 1 problem." He could have just said, I think the cable is broken. Here is the primer on OSI:

OSI Model (http://schl.mn/bacis07)

CISSP DOMAINS

I will talk about certifications coming up. The ten domains that make up the CISSP actually make for a great outline on key concepts you should understand in information security.

The domains can be found here (http://schl.mn/bacis08). This is a great outline for learning. In your first year, you should make it a goal to read or learn something from each of the ten domains. This is a great way to make yourself more well-rounded.

REGULATIONS

There are actually too many regulations to recommend any one person to read. Depending upon what industry you want to work in or are working in, there are specific regulations to consider. I have outlined the most common by industry below. Read and understand the regulations specific to where you work.

Financial Service

- GLBA - Gramm–Leach–Bliley Act
- PCI - Payment Card Industry Compliance
- SOX - Sarbanes Oxley (as it related to access)

Energy

- NERC

- FERC

Healthcare

- HIPAA
- HITECH

US Government

- FISMA
- FedRamp
- Various NIST guidance

FRAMEWORKS

Often confused as a regulation are a few frameworks that are very helpful in understanding security.

ISO 27001 and 27002

ISO 27001 is the standard for building an information security program. Mirroring the ten CISSP domains, 27001 outlines capabilities an information security organization should have and the controls which should be in place. You can be certified against the ISO standard (not many organizations do). Read more here (http://schl.mn/bacis09).

NIST 800-53

Without trying hard, you'll hear people reference high, medium and low risks to the organization. The idea of managing information security risk ties back to a NIST document, NIST 800-53 (http://schl.mn/bacis010). It is a rich document outlining how to manage controls, risks, and specifically how you calculate whether a risk is high, medium or low to the organization.

READING

Most of the information above is so core to information security, I should never have to update the content. It was many of the core pieces of information I learned 20 years ago as I started my career.

As you can imagine, information security moves so fast that information can become dated quickly. While you should make sure you understand the core information, you should constantly be reading. Read blogs, books, newspapers, whatever you can get your hands on. I put together a weekly newsletter with the latest long-form information security articles each Friday. You can sign up for that here: (http://schl.mn/bacis011).

CERTIFICATIONS

My full analysis of certifications is contained in this blog post:

https://www.jayschulman.com/the-only-security-certifications-you-actually-need/

Here is what you need to know:

There are a few reasons to get a certification: 1) get a raise/promotion, 2) get a new job, 3) prove you have the skills (which likely ties back to 1 and 2).

For most security professionals, the CISSP is a very beneficial certification. It's important to note that most big companies use basic searching algorithms to eliminate candidates. Don't have the CISSP? You're not qualified. (You're probably incredibly qualified but unfortunately it's too hard for them to figure that out.)

The only other certification that I would recommend is if you're in the auditing space. The CISA is still a very common certification (representing likely half of security jobs posted). Given its auditing slant, it's not for everyone.

My recommendations are based on an analysis for people who are looking to make themselves more marketable to future employers. There are some great certifications that are not only valuable but incredibly difficult to pass. The truth though is that not a lot of employers are looking for people with a particular certification. That said, they are likely looking for people with those skill sets. A particular certification might make it easier for you to prove you have that skill.

Finally, no certification replaces actual on the ground knowledge you learn day-to-day. While these certifications are good checkboxes, ultimately it's how you communicate your knowledge during various interview processes.

MANAGING YOUR FIRST YEAR

Do not skip this section because you are not in your first year. My guidance is recommended as anyone moves from a novice to a mature information security professional.

Start Broad

I have met many people starting off in their information security career who just wanted to be penetration testers. We are about 2000 words into this book and this is the first I have mentioned pentesting.

That is certainly the glamorous side of information security. *Hacking* into computer systems. For a long time, even though I was not an active pentester, when people asked what I did for a living I would say "hacker."

If you have a desire to grow beyond pentesting, now is your opportunity to broaden your skillset.

I recommend that you try to create the broadest information security experience you can in your first few years. I have a couple of key reasons:

- There are plenty of interesting security jobs that you may never know about unless you open your mind to the full suite of information security.
- As opportunities open up in your organization or others, they may not be in your area. If you've experienced others, you have a greater likelihood of moving up in that other area.
- It makes you a more well-rounded professional. The more you know, the easier it will be to grow your career.

What does this mean practically? Do not turn down the opportunity to do something because it is not in your core skillset. Try to attend as many meetings, trainings, and other events to learn as much as you can -- both inside your organization and in the security community.

If you attend conferences, stop off at presentations that are out of your core skillset to see what others are doing.

Tips on Helping You Learn

How many times have you sat down determined to learn something new, but given up before you have reached your goal? I am often asked, "When did you learn..." or "How do you know how to..." My blog at JaySchulman.com has been a big part of my platform to learn for the past two years.

A Platform for Learning

If you asked me why I blog, I will probably come up with one of 9 different excuses for why I do it. Branding, I enjoy writing, outlet for expression. The reality is that over the past two years, I have learned more through the process of running a blog than I have about actually writing the blog itself.

A History of My Platform for Learning

Two years ago I decided to get *serious* about blogging. I have probably only posted a dozen times in 2 years. Serious usually means building a new site, changing platforms, changing hosting providers. Here is a quick summary of the tech refreshes I have done in the past year and -- most importantly -- the technology I have learned doing it:

- Wordpress on AWS EC2 (running on a single EC2 instance)
- Wordpress on AWS EC2 with RDS (running the database on Amazon's DB offering)
- Jekyll (Rails blogging platform) on Heroku
- Ghost (Node.JS) on Heroku
- Wordpress on Openshift (Red Hat's Platform as a Service)
- Wordpress on Google's App Engine (as part of a bigger shift to try Google's cloud offering)

These points do not factor in all of the pieces and parts that go into running a blog (plugins, search engine optimization, etc).

Translate that into technology stacks I learned:

- **Cloud Providers**: AWS, Google, Heroku, Openshift
- **Languages**: PHP, Rails, Node.js
- **Number of Total Posts**: 12

Find an Excuse to Learn

If I had sat down to *learn* Amazon's Web Services platform, I probably would have started up couple of services, played around, but not really understood how the platform comes together. In building out jayschulman.com on AWS, I learned:

- EC2 - the compute instance that runs the Wordpress Code
- RDS - the shared database product
- Cloudfront - Amazon's content delivery network
- S3 - Amazon's storage product
- Route 53 - Amazon's Domain Name Hosting product
- SES - Amazon's e-mail sending service

In setting up and troubleshooting a real website, I understand better how each of the components comes together.

You should try this kind of learning too. Instead of sitting down with a book on the topic you want to learn, find a project that uses that topic. Want to learn Node.js? Find something that you need or want developed and use Node for that project. If you have a specific attainable goal, it is easier to build your learnings to meet that goal.

The problem with understanding big topics -- like a programming language or technologies -- is that it is so broad that it is hard to make it meaningful unless you have an end goal. Make a useful end goal and then build a learning plan on meeting that goal.

Jay, how are my *hobbies* going to help me at work?

They may seem like hobbies today, but it is amazing how they will intertwine with your everyday life.

In information security, it is funny how often my *hobby projects* overlap with my work life. Especially with something like Amazon Web Services, they come up all the time. And it is not about being an expert in the area, but understanding enough that it makes sense to apply to security. A number of my clients use AWS and simply being able to understand whether they are using VPCs (Virtual Private Connections) is immensely helpful.

For Pleasure, Not for Work

In interviews, I often ask the question "What are you passionate about? What do you play with at home after hours?" The idea is that I am looking for your creative juices. If the answer is, "blogging," great! That's a foundation to learn a lot beyond what I am expecting 9 to 5.

Build your project with learning and enjoyment in mind, not with a specific work goal. You will have a greater chance for success and you will be free to pivot where the project takes you. If my goal was to learn AWS, I would have been less likely to pivot to Heroku, Google, etc.

Interviewing

It is not unusual to get a phone call from a friend with a great opportunity but something is holding them back from going on the interview. When I ask why are you hesitant to interview, I get one of the following responses:

- ☐ I think I'm getting a promotion at work soon.
- ☐ They want me to relocate.
- ☐ The commute isn't good.

In essence, they have already played out the scenario in their head of what it would be like to work at that company -- and yet they've never walked in the door.

Unless your current employer will find out that you interviewed, I generally encourage people to take the interview. Here's why.

1. Truth from Fiction

You have this image of the company in your head. Maybe you have romanticized it. Snacks in the cafeteria. Flexible work hours. Really cool projects. That is all conjecture. Until you get in there, understand the job, culture, and who you'd be working for, you have no idea what it is going to be like.

Many years ago, I interviewed at Playboy for a job as their first security administrator. Back in 2000, walking into Playboy was like walking into another world. The interviews were fun. The people were great. Then came the heart-to-heart. "Jay, we're built upon the first amendment. Any restrictions you'd like to implement here will need the approval of Christie Hefner."

Fact is, they were not ready for a security administrator to lock them down. A year later, they were hacked, see: (http://schl.mn/bacis012). It would be hard to accept a job as a powerless security administrator.

If I had not taken the Playboy interviews, I would always think how great it would have been to work there. Instead, I interviewed and understood it was not the place for me.

2. Practice Makes Perfect

When is the last time you interviewed? If it has been a while, you are probably rusty. You forgot your stock answers to "Where do you see yourself in five years?" There are very few everyday circumstances that mimic a job interview. So to get practice, go on more interviews!

In fact, talk to every recruiter that calls you up. Each call you take you will get more experience answering those questions. "Why are you thinking of leaving?" You will get better at telling them what you want in a job and figuring out what will make you happy.

That way, the day the recruiter calls with the ultimate gig, you will sound great and be ready to interview.

3. You Are Looking At The Wrong Things

Back to my first point, you have already run through this in your head. The company is an extra 30 minute drive and you hate driving. You heard they have the cubes with the low walls so it is going to be loud.

Turns out that is all true, but the people who work there are great. It is loud because everyone is having a good time. They want to train you on 3 new things and you are going to work on their next generation product. No one gets in until 10a and leaves at 6p. That kind of work atmosphere can make the extra drive time worth it.

You think you know what you like because of what you have today. You have a short commute so a longer commute must be bad. Turns out you love audiobooks -- which makes the drive feel shorter.

The company may still not be right for you, but seeing what other companies have to offer gives you a better perspective of what you really want.

What's most important:

You have to be happy in your job. Talking to recruiters, talking to companies, and talking to your friends gives you the opportunity to learn what you really like so you will know the right job when it comes around.

Pick Your Boss, Not Your Job

A friend called me to say he was leaving his current job. His boss was unbearable. A recruiter I commonly network with often tells me that the number one reason he's able to pull people out of great companies is bad bosses.

As a consultant, I have the opportunity to talk with people in a variety of companies at a variety of levels. I can usually tell by talking to the employee whether they have a good boss.

I believe that good bosses can bring the best out of their team. The following are two key criteria good bosses display. You can see from the examples the impact a good boss can have on your career.

Manage

I hope you chuckle. It is amazing how many managers do not actually manage. They typically project manage. Are you getting the things done we need you to get done? They are not providing the direction or background to make you successful.

Here is a classic example of good managing versus bad:

The Bad Manager

The bad manager tells you that the business is looking into cloud computing. *Go figure out what they need and make sure it fits into our standards.*

The Good Manager

The good manager provides the context to make you successful. *The business is looking to provide this new capability. They think the cloud will help them do that. The CEO said the other day we have to get to market before our competitor. Can you help the business figure out whether this cloud service will do that?*

Especially in information security, we use the context of generic security rather than what the business is trying to accomplish. It is the difference between saying no and trying to understand how you can help the business achieve what they need to achieve securely.

Coach

This is where I believe good managers can become great managers. Going back to our cloud computing example:

I often tell people early on in their career that there is going to be a point where it is more important to learn the business than the technology. In the above example, the manager provides the context. As a coach, it is an opportunity to help the employee grow. *While you are there, you will be more successful in the long term if you build relationships with the business and learn what they do.*

The idea of coaching is long-term, not short-term. Investing in your employees will pay dividends in the future.

This is Basic Stuff

It is. I am embarrassed to write it and yet I would guess more than 50% of you have bad bosses. You are getting no guidance and no coaching. (If you are a bad boss, unfortunately I cannot fix it for you 700 words.)

How You Can Help Your Boss (and you)

My hunch is that many bad bosses have the talent to manage and coach but do not make the time to do it. If it is the difference between finishing a project for their boss or giving you advice, they are focused up the ladder and not down.

There are bosses that are plain bad. Move on.

For those who have potential, help them out:

Think about a survey you would fill out about your boss. *Does he/she give timely feedback? Do they inform you of important corporate decisions?*

Start asking those questions. *How am I doing? How do you think that project turned out? I saw a reorganization in department A, what was behind that?*

Many years ago, I tried this technique with a plain bad boss. *"Jay, I'm not exactly sure how you're doing. How do you think you're doing?"*

You may have a great job with an awful boss. It happens. Hopefully some of the tips above can help salvage that relationship.

What Do You Do?

I'm fascinated by the various answers I get when I ask someone "What do you do?"

It should be a simple question but their answer says so much about who they are. Most of the answers can be put into two buckets.

I am a...

With this answer, their job descriptions defines them. I am a consultant. I build automobiles. My favorite example is from Winston Wolf (http://schl.mn/bacis013). "I solve problems."

I work for...

Here, they put more pride in who they work for than what they do. I work for the city. I'm with JPMorganChase. It does not matter what they do, they do it for this company.

You are your answer

What do you do? Most people do not think about their answer until asked the question. It is important to think about how you think about your job description and the company you work for. The answer to this question is your personal brand. It is important to me to have a personal brand -- it should be important to you.

Throughout my career, I have answered the question in different ways. Early in my career, I said *I hack into computers.* Not only did I feel like that defined me, it was a simple answer everyone could understand. (It also sounded cooler than security consultant.)

I switched when I worked for JPMorganChase. I took great pride in working for JPMC. Given the bank's philanthropy along with Jamie Dimon's stump speech on technology defining the bank, I was proud of who I worked for.

Today, I generally answer with *I help companies fix their security issues.* It is probably no less defining than, "I hack into computers," but shows a more mature view of the industry. I also want to emphasize that I want to help fix the problem, not just find them.

We used to call it an elevator pitch. Today it is your twitter headline. You only have about 15 seconds to lock someone's attention. As a consultant, I use my pitch all the time -- and vary it for my audience. Even if you work internally for a company, new co-workers often ask the question. Are you in the Widgets Department or are you in charge of widgets.

FIND A MENTOR

In the early days of my security career, everyone told you to find a mentor but no one really did. I would hear friends say they had a "mentor" but it was really just someone they were modeling their career after.

I cannot say that I went out and interviewed a bunch of people to be mentors -- I just fell into them. They were bosses who were no longer my boss. They were people I just talked to regularly for advice or a few people who would reach out to me to check in on how I was doing (see: Find a Mentee http://schl.mn/bacis014 in Chapter 3).

I am the kind of guy who thinks he has figured it all out. In hindsight, explaining my next steps -- even if it is just to hear how it sounds when I try to explain it to someone else -- is very powerful.

My past mentors have tweaked my ideas, told me when to be aggressive and passive and connected dots that I could not see.

Connecting those dots is what I try to do as a mentor myself. When you are in the middle of an issue, it is hard to see the big picture. Mentors are great at outlining what they see and recommend a few steps forward. Especially when I have doubted myself, mentors gave me the confidence to push through.

How Do You Pick A Mentor?

Carefully. Here are a couple of recommendations I have on picking a good mentor:

- **They should not be the mirror image of you in 5 years.** You want someone who is going to challenge you, provide a different perspective. If all of your advice is the same advice you'd give, then you're not getting good advice.
- **Someone who has the same philosophy as you.** I call this book a philosophy. When I pick a mentor, I'm looking for someone who believes a lot of the things I write about. What is your philosophy on security and your career?
- **Someone headed in the direction you want to go.** If you want to be a CISO, find a CISO or someone on their way to being a CISO. If you want to be a security researcher, find a researcher as a mentor. Part of

being a good mentor is helping them not repeat the same mistakes you made. If you are both going down the same path, your mentor can help you through the same huddles they faced.

☐ **Set expectations.** How often should you catch up? Phone? Video? In Person? How do you want the conversations to go? All of these basic question should be established so you do not go into the relationship thinking you will talk weekly and they only have time to talk quarterly.

WRAPPING UP YEAR 1

As I described this chapter in the beginning, it is a foundational chapter. The next chapter is a Security Bootcamp. It lists approximately 20 areas of security and provides links to open source tools or information so you can dig in on each topic.

CHAPTER 2. SECURITY BOOTCAMP

Security is such a broad topic. It means different things to different people. In picking up this book, my guess is that you know some of the 14 disciplines and 12 tools listed below. I would challenge you to broaden your knowledge and start learning in areas that you do not already know. My goal of this chapter is not to teach you all 26 *things* but to give you a quick background on each and provide some references for learning more about each area.

SECURITY DISCIPLINES

1. Security Architecture

Security Architecture is an often overlooked art in information security. We too often cobble a couple of tools together to make something work instead of thinking through how the pieces fit together.

Security architecture is sometimes part of information security and can also be embedded in the overall enterprise architecture functionality. Either way, the goal is to evaluate infrastructure, applications, and other areas of the enterprise to ensure the pieces are put together in a secure manner.

The Open Security Architecture group (http://schl.mn/bacis015) is a great place to start for more information.

2. Compliance

I would not even know where to start with compliance. There is a laundry list of regulations and compliance requirements that apply to information security. I would do two things to brush up on compliance. 1) Understand the full spectrum of regulations in the area at a high level. 2)

Actually read and understand the specific regulations that apply to the industry you work in (or consult in).

While this is outdated by three years or so, it is actually one of the better resources out there. Check out CSO Online's list of infosec regulations here (http://schl.mn/bacis016).

3. Forensics

I put forensics in the disciplines section because it is in fact a discipline. But to really learn and understand it, you should practice with a tool. (That feels like a no-no.)

With a lot of things in this list, they are preventative. You do them to stop a security issue from occurring. With Forensics, it's detective. You're looking for a problem after it happened. These tools are great for playing. Go find an old hard drive and try to figure out what is recoverable, what you were last doing, and what interesting information you can find. **Do not** actually try this for real. If you ever want to prosecute someone, you need chain of custody and the preservation of the original image (you make an exact duplicate). Try out:

The Sleuth Kit/Autopsy Browser

The Sleuth Kit is a command-line tool, and the Autopsy Browser provides a graphical front-end to make it easier to use. The site also offers quite a bit of information about digital forensics in general.

4. Vendor Assessments

Vendor assessments are the pain of most information security organizations. Either you have to fill out too many or you can never contact enough vendors.

Every organization has its own approach to assessing the security of vendors. There was a thought that we could all agree on a single framework and save a bunch of time by not filling out different forms each week. That idea has not been widely adopted, but the artifacts are quite strong. Go to sharedassessments.org (http://schl.mn/bacis019) to learn about the concept and download the spreadsheet here (http://schl.mn/bacis021), to read through the entire shared vendor assessment. It's a great place to understand the overall concepts.

5. Risk Assessments

There are as many risk assessment frameworks as there are vendor assessment questionnaires but the gold standard is NIST 800-30. (Even if you aren't US-based, the document is rich with information.)

It is a really detailed read, but it will give you just about everything you need to understand risk assessment methodologies. Check out:

SP 800-30 Rev. 1	Sep 2012	**Guide for Conducting Risk Assessments** SP 800-30 Rev. 1 (http://schl.mn/bacis022) SP 800-30 Rev. 1 (EPUB) (http://schl.mn/bacis23)

6. Awareness

Security Awareness is one of the hardest areas of information security to be effective. No matter what you do, you are at the whim of a human. Security awareness is the practice of helping humans (we could also call them employees, students, whomever you are tasked with protecting) understand information security and make good security decisions. It is no wonder one of the best (and open source) resource on the topic is called Securing the Human (http://schl.mn/bacis024).

7. Governance

At the top of the information security organization is where governance is applied. In fact, the governance in many organizations includes the board of directors or other risk committees to ensure security is getting the right attention within the company.

It is a complex and often controversial topic among both security people and executives. (Who should the CISO report to is usually the most argued.)

Start by reading this publication from ISACA on the topic here (http://schl.mn/bacis025). If it interests you, read through the references in the document for a long list of other great reads on the topic.

8. Policy

Right under governance is policy. I wrote a blog post about how we have too many policies (http://schl.mn/bacis026) that is worth a read. The best way to understand policy is to read through policies. While there is definitely an art and a science to policy writing, it is important to consider an organization's culture as well. My story of turning down a security job at Playboy (http://schl.mn/bacis027) is directly related to Playboy's culture around policies.

Check out SANS's policy resource center here (http://schl.mn/bacis028) for a library of common security policies.

9. Identity Management

A few years ago, I was talking with a CFO who asked me the question "Why is adding and removing users so hard? This seems like it should be easy." The best place to start learning about IAM is this old article here (http://schl.mn/bacis029) design for internal auditors.

10. Incident Management

It is not that an incident occurred; it is how you handle it. Check out this in-depth guide to incident management here (http://schl.mn/bacis030), written by the European Union Agency for Network and Information Security.

11. Threat Intelligence

Threat Intelligence is all of the information that is accumulated to determine the who, what, when, and where an attack may occur. Threat information can be very expensive to buy. The best free resource in through SANS. It is called the Internet Storm Center see: (http://schl.mn/bacis031).

12. Application Security

Let me preface application security with this caveat: It is hard for a developer to take advice from a security person if they have never developed code. If you want to pursue a career in application security, make sure you write code.

Then read the Building Security In Maturity Model here (http://schl.mn/bacis032). It is definitely a comprehensive view of everything that encompasses the application security space.

13. Vulnerability Management

I like to say that Vulnerability Management is the art of fixing vulnerabilities in your environment. Truth is that it is the entire lifecycle of finding, fixing, and reporting on the issues in your environment. A PDF from SANS is a good starting point, found here (http://schl.mn/bacis033).

14. Business Continuity/Disaster Recovery

This is a lost art. Often abbreviated BCDR, very modern companies (think Twitter and Facebook) opt for high-availability instead of disaster recovery. The basis of Amazon Web Services Availability Zones is the idea that you can place your data and services in so many different locations that you'll never go down. Then again, that is the core foundation of business continuity. Start with the Wikipedia article here (http://schl.mn/bacis034) as a good foundation for the practices.

SECURITY TOOLS

1. Content Filtering

DansGuardian (http://schl.mn/bacis035) is a network content filtering tool which uses phrase matching, PICS filtering and URL filtering to help block objectionable content.

I do not think content filtering fits into the security eco-system anymore. It did when I was growing up but now it is become more of a standard infrastructure function. Regardless, if it intrigues you, this is worth playing with.

2. Antivirus

ClamAV (http://schl.mn/bacis036) is known as "the de facto standard for mail gateway scanning." ClamAV is one of the most popular open source security applications available.

A lot of people consider Antivirus part of the security function. I do not. I think it is another standard infrastructure tool.

3. Malware

Malware is interesting. For detection, the tool you want to checkout is Malwarebytes here (http://schl.mn/bacis037). Again, that is more standard infrastructure than security. The analysis of what malware does, that is pure security. That typically is part of the forensics capability. Jump up there and load up the Forensics Toolkit found here (http://schl.mn/bacis038) as a start.

4. Web Application Firewall

Web Application Firewalls or WAFs are just a fancier way of filtering bad web requests. Quick soapbox: WAFs should not be used to protect otherwise vulnerable applications. Fix the code!

That said, WAFs can take the load off the webservers for the well-known, easy to block non-sense that people try. The open-source standard is ModSecurity found here (http://schl.mn/bacis039). It is definitely worth playing with in a sandbox.

5. Intrusion Prevention/Detection (IPS/IDS)

Luckily, our home internet connections are so full of internet security non-sense that playing with an IPS/IDS is actually pretty easy to do at home. Go download Suricata IDS here (http://schl.mn/bacis040) and load it up against your cable modem or even put it in a virtual machine and take it to your local free WiFi and see what's going on with the network. Fun for the entire family!

6. PKI/Encryption

PKI is a tough one to try out at home. You probably do not run a visitor system at your front door to register guests into your directory. The best I could come up with was connecting my WiFi to a Radius server which used OpenCA found here (http://schl.mn/bacis041) and OpenLDAP found here (http://schl.mn/bacis042) as the backend. Definitely a complicated setup but I learned a lot.

Gnu Privacy Guard (GPG) (http://schl.mn/bacis043) is the email encryption solution to try out. It supports multiple encryption algorithms and offers good key management features. It is also super easy to try out although as XKCD joked aboutt here (http://schl.mn/bacis044), no one ever asks you for your PGP key.

7. Data Loss Prevention (DLP)

Here is another one to throw on your home network and see what it picks up. OpenDLP (http://schl.mn/bacis045) is a centrally managed DLP solution that can scan thousands of Windows or Unix systems at once to discover any sensitive data at rest. Want something more robust? Try MyDLP found here (http://schl.mn/bacis046). MyDLP can actually prevent sensitive data from leaving your system as well as identifying its location.

8. Multi-Factor Authentication

Two options for MFA at home. Duo Security (http://schl.mn/bacis047) is a leader in the multi-factor authentication space and they offer a free version for home use. Install it on your home machines to try it out. It is rock solid. You are relying upon a SaaS app, though. That is not *really* home brew. If you want to setup everything from scratch, go with linotp found here (http://schl.mn/bacis048).

9. Log Collection/Aggregation

Splunk is the commercial leader in the log aggregation space. Graylog, found here (http://schl.mn/bacis049) is the open source equivalent. Unless you are running a LOT of systems at home, log aggregation is not too exciting. You never know what you can correlate between your cable modem, wifi, and home theater PC.

10. Static Code

The fine folks at OWASP did all the work for me. Since static code analysis is language dependant and many tools work only for a few languages, the options here are endless. Follow this link for a full listing of just about every static tool (free and paid) you can imagine: **http://schl.mn/bacis050**

11. Dynamic Scanning

OWASP again is providing a wealth of different free and paid for tools to look for application vulnerabilities via a dynamic scan: **http://schl.mn/bacis051**

SUMMARY

Remember, the objective with all of these tools is to broaden your skillset. I'm a big believer that you really understand the technology when you get your hands dirty. Each of these tools above give you a chance to find something interesting and new to study.

Chapter 3. Year 1

By the time you get to your first anniversary, I hope the foundational knowledge in the Day 1 chapter has set in. Are you experienced in all of the areas in the last chapter? No way. Hopefully you understand the principles and are thinking through how they apply to you.

Year 1 talks a lot about management. How to be a great manager. If you learn to be a manager when you are a manager, it will be a rough start. Start learning the foundations today and you'll excel your career greatly.

Learn To Manage

At some point in your career, you make the jump from doing stuff to managing people who do stuff. Many times it is before you have the term *manager* in your title. More often than not, you still do a bunch of stuff while delegating others to help you do those things.

Everyone has a different management style. Everyone wants to be managed differently. I do not think there is a right way to be a manager but I do think there are two ways to figure out what kind of manager you should be.

Find Someone You Respect and Follow Them

Hopefully you have seen a few people *manage*. It is even better if you have had a bunch of managers. What did you like about each of them? How was it to be managed by them? (If it was not a good experience, wait for option #2.)

In the consulting business, you end up with a bunch of managers. I have heard the term matrix management -- you report to a bunch of people at the same time. As a result, I have been able to see a variety of management techniques to pick and choose what I saw working.

Early on in my career, I met Gary who greatly influenced the manager that I am today. He fought for his employees, he always remained calm no matter the stress of the situation, and that reflected in the team that he managed.

Often when I am in a new management situation, I think back to, "*What would Gary do?*"

Find An Ineffective Manager and Do The Opposite

When we first promote people to manager, I often see an odd effect. There are a group of new managers who decide to fix all of the ways they were managed poorly and a group of people who -- much like hazing -- want to treat their team the same way they were treated.

I do not agree with the latter. As new managers, you have an opportunity to change the culture and build a stronger team. Think about the poor management characteristics and change them. If you believe that you are managing the way you would want to be managed, your team should appreciate it.

LEARN TO SELL

I hear often of a common barrier for security people. "I have trouble selling my security program." I usually hear it when a security person has outstanding ideas and plans but they cannot get anyone else in their organization to believe in or fund them.

That is because they are not thinking of themselves as a salesperson.

How We Are All Salespeople

If you come from a consulting background, you already think about selling. When a consultant jumps to an internal organization, all of the sudden they forget about sales. In your part of a security organization, you are always selling.

You need to sell your boss, sell your budget holders, and sell your organizations on your ideas.

How CFOs Understand Security

I had the opportunity a few years ago to talk with the CFO of a major fast food chain. He was concerned about security -- specifically about how they were managing users in the system. He had heard the security team talk about how they needed a lot of money to fix the problem. They showed him PowerPoint decks, analysis and proposals on how much it would cost to fix the problem. Ultimately he asked the question: Why is this so complicated?

With all of the detail he was provided, the security team never answered that question. In very simple terms, I explained to the CFO the complexities managing users across multiple systems. He got it and he signed off on a project to fix the problem.

Sell Your Neighbor

We all have a neighbor that asks what we do and is completely lost when you describe your security job. Think about what you are trying to accomplish and think about how you would explain it to your neighbor. Jargon? Make sure it is out or clearly explained. Did you establish the problem? What is obvious to you is not always obvious to your neighbor.

And finally, think about how your favorite salesperson would sell it.

Listen To Professional Sales People

Think about the last time a salesperson walked into your office, pulled out a deck, walked through all of the companies who are using their product.You probably zoned out. Next time, consider it a teaching moment. Listen to how they take complex technology and distill it into something easy to comprehend. (Here's hoping they are a good salesperson.) Take those skills with you as you internally try to sell your own projects and ideas.

The best security people -- and the best Chief Information Security Officers -- are those that can help those around them understand the problem and get them to believe in the solution. I will talk more about CISOs in Chapter 3.

THE ONLY 2 THINGS YOU NEED TO BE A GREAT MANAGER

Many years ago I was in an internal meeting. It was one of those annual meetings where we talking about the year ahead, problems we have faced, and how to overcome them. Apparently, in the prior year, we spent too much time asking for permission before executing. I am guessing it is a common problem in many organizations.

Our leader, whose leadership style I have tried to emulate, laid out a plan to allow more independent thinking. He outlined ten *facts* that we could follow. That was twelve years ago. In the past twelve years, I have realized that I only need to follow the first two. (It appears the next 8 all can be rolled into either the first two.)

Note: This is written using the term "client." I have been a consultant for the better part of 15 years. If you are not serving an outside *client*, you probably have an internal client.

1. Take Care of Your Clients

If you had the choice between grabbing lunch with your client and anyone else, grab it with your client. This seems simple and yet in a given week, we probably do not always put them first. There are two primary ways to take care of your clients:

As a function of time management, we can not get everything done in a given day, week, or year. The idea is that if you had a choice between helping a client or working on an internal project, the client should come first. Take a look at your priorities today. How many of them are directly impacting the clients you serve?

Often clients come with a difficult problem that needs solving. Can we execute a project differently? Can we get a new/different resource? Find a way to solve their problem or meet their needs. We cannot always say, "Yes," to every client request, but are we advocating for them to get them the best we can do?

If you think back to the last month, have you put your clients first?

2. Take Care of The People Who Take Care of Your Clients

In the consulting business, I often see consulting managers get the first one right but miss the second. They go hand in hand. If you do not have a team, who is going to take care of your clients? In a three person consulting team -- one manager and two consultants -- the client probably sees more of the consultants then the manager. They are the front facing part of your organization. Think about the following scenarios:

What is the impact of giving a consultant a day off after working a 60 hour week?

Think about the trickle down effect of empowering a consultant.

Imagine the impact of saying "thank you."

We should always take care of our people. When you frame it as a direct link to the service of your client or customer, it becomes a key link to a successful business. Think about the negative:

The effect turnover has on your client projects.

How apparent an unhappy consultant is to your client.

How unmotivated a consultant could be in solving your client's needs.

Now Think of Everything Else

In any given day, my to-do list is filled with items that have nothing to do with my clients or the people that serve them. Itis important to me to make sure those items do not impact my ability to take care of my clients and the people who serve them.

As you reframe your priorities, keep in mind that I was not able to change my priorities overnight. Even today, an internal project or something that does not fit into these two buckets can take me away from my core priorities. Understanding that these are the two most important goals has helped me keep my focus over the long term.

THE TRANSITION FROM TECH TO EXEC

In the early part of your career, you are rewarded for your technology skills. As you grow into a manager, those skills begin to fade and your ability to communicate those skills and ideas begins to rise.

Watch Your Words

The very first CISO I met -- probably around 2003 -- could have used this advice. We were sitting in a meeting with the CFO trying to explain how the company was going to tackle PCI. PCI had just come out. It was actually not yet a very big deal.

The CISO got down into the weeds really fast on how they had to <insert long list of acronyms and super tech stuff>. The CFO responded, "Why do we need to do this?" A person on the CFO's team started explaining the principles of PCI and how their bank was going to fine them if they did not comply. The CFO got it and put that person in charge of the project.

When issues occur in security, as professionals we are very passionate to get it accurate. It is not just a "web request" but HTML over port 80. It is not "in the URL" but a GET request.

Yep, you definitely need to understand all of the acronyms, tech lingo, and if randomly quizzed in the hall be able to recite configurations flags in NMAP.

When you are not talking to an information security professional, make sure they understand what you are saying.

In journalism, they call it *dumbing it down.* Journalists write as if they are talking to a first grader because it ensures everything they are saying can be completely understood by anyone who picks up the article.

Your ability to explain complex technology to people who do not understand it is **highly** valued. It is critical if you want to become a CISO.

(Yeah, I know Chapter 3 is about the Executive Security role but this is probably one of the harder concepts to learn. Start early on this one.)

FIND A MENTEE

Earlier in the book, I recommended you find a mentor. You may have found that easy to do or hard. A lot of people ask me where to find mentors.

Mentoring is a give and take relationship. We need just as many mentors as mentees. If you're only taking (having a mentor), it's also important to have a mentee. You may not do this right away, but somewhere at the mid-point in your career, you should have one (or more).

Besides just giving back, having a mentee gives you a new perspective on the security community. Specifically for me, it was very helpful in creating my views on managing millennials (saving that for another book) and understanding other people's perspectives. As you grow up, you have a tendency to view the world as if it hasn't changed. Being a mentor helps correct or re-frame that view.

CHAPTER 4. YEAR 10

This is the first in a series of books on Building your Life and Career in Security. Year 10 is about growing into the role of a

Chief Information Security Officer or Principal Security Professional.

The next book will focus on the CISO role itself. This chapter is designed to help you grow into that role. There are three key components to growing into the executive role:

1. Understand the Business
2. Communicate the Risks
3. Grow Your Team

You would not think the CISO role was that easy.

UNDERSTAND THE BUSINESS

Please do not think this section is about researching a company you want to work for before you interview. This is about understanding how your particular organization makes money. How is your revenue generated,? How are your expenses calculated? How does technology enable the business?

As security people, we often find it easiest to say no. If you were at General Motors when they were creating OnStar (the cellular enabled emergency and assistance service built-in to GM vehicles), you might say, "No, we don't want to create a network connection from the internet to the vehicle."

Understand the business. OnStar is a recurring revenue product. After you have purchased the car, you keep paying GM for the service. Additionally, it provides a wealth of data to understand how the car is used. Something that will help GM make cars better. By understanding your business, you hopefully would look at OnStar differently. It is not, "No, you can't do that." It is, "How can we make sure that no one can use the cellular connection to access the car or our network?"

Another example is a stock or options exchange. Trades are transacted at the speed of light (or faster). If you think about the foundations of security -- Confidentiality, Integrity, and Availability (called the CIA) -- your return on investment for confidentiality is pretty low. The value of a transaction is very, very short (think seconds). So encrypting the transaction does not make sense. In fact, trying to encrypt the transaction at the speed of light may in fact allow traders to play with the encryption to game the system.

So instead, focus on integrity and availability.

Back to my core point, you need all of this information to understand not only how you should be securing the environment but what is the impact of the controls you might put in place.

COMMUNICATE THE RISKS

You can be the best security guy this side of the city, but if you cannot communicate, you will never get what you need.

Communication is not about technical accuracy. Communication is not about instilling fear, uncertainty, or doubt. Communication is about understanding the business (as described above) and being able to communicate in a way the business can understand what the risks are and what your recommended mitigation is to those risks.

It also means giving your executive team the ability to understand the overall risks to the organization and how they are changing over time (let's call that metrics). If you are explaining your metrics in security terms (such as vulnerabilities) then you not only have to explain the numbers but what the numbers stand for.

In college, I took a lot of communications courses (it is no wonder; I enjoy writing and speaking). One of the key concepts is to write (or speak) for your audience. I know as security people we hate to do it, but sometimes it makes sense to dumb down the issues.

Quick example:

There is a SQL Injection in your web application which allows an attacker to pull down the password table which is salted and hashed.

Technically accurate but your CFO who needs to authorize spending to fix it probably does not get it. Try this instead:

A user on the internet can download all of our users passwords by creating a specially crafted URL. Luckily our passwords are protected through an industry standard encryption mechanism.

Yeah, it definitely does not sound as cool but the CFO walks away understanding 1) anyone can do this, 2) it is bad but not horribly bad because we are doing something industry standard and 3) we should fix it.

This is remedial third grade advice, Jay

If you ask anyone how they should be communicating, they will for the most part agree that you need to make it understandable. I continue to see two scenarios:

The Correction

Usually it starts with the non-security guy trying to repeat back the scenario in their own terms. Then someone chimes in trying to explain the nuance. Maybe it is the details around how the injection occurs. Maybe it is something specific to the platform. Whatever it is, it is muddying up the waters. Use the KISS principle (Keep It Simple Stupid).

The Heat of the Moment

I typically see this around breaches (or suspected breaches which are false alarms). You call the war room. Everyone gathers. Then someone pops up a screenshot of Splunk, Wireshark, Burp. Maybe it is because they have not had time to think through how to present the information. Maybe it is back to needing accuracy under a breach-type situation. All I see are a bunch of non-security people trying to understand a cryptic screenshot of something they really do not need to understand.

Point made. When in doubt, KISS.

GROW YOUR TEAM

There are a set of security people who I presume are great people to have working for you, but awful people to work for. Sometimes they are identified early on as bad managers and put in positions where they are not responsible for a team. Unfortunately sometimes they are left to manage.

You can do everything in this book to the letter. Skip this last point and you will be calling me up going, "Dude, it's not working."

The first thing you should do every day is make sure take care of your clients (whether that is your boss, the business, or if you are a consultant it is the actual client). The next thing to do is make sure to take care of the people who take care of your clients. That is your team (and your team's team, etc).

There are a couple of reasons why this is so important:

- ◻ You need an empowered and motivated team to tackle the impossible task of securing your environment.
- ◻ As of 2016, security people are in high demand. If you are not a good boss, they will find one (in another company) elsewhere.
- ◻ The problem starts to compound when you cannot get new people to backfill the people who left.

SUMMARY

Again, this chapter isn't the manual to being a CISO. It's a few foundational steps that make the difference between being a functional CISO and an executive CISO. (I have a blog post here on the 7 different types of CISOs.)

Chapter 5. Where To Go From Here

Thanks for getting this far in the book. (Please do not tell me you clicked on the Table of Contents and jumped here first.)

The life of an information security professional is ever changing. As I went through the editing process, I would change things as I felt it was no longer relevant. And I wrote this in months, not years.

So books are not the greatest medium for keeping up to date on security. That is why a built a platform for growing your security career.

Books

I am committed to continuing publishing books on your security career. While it is ever changing, it is also a great medium to really dig into a subject. You can follow my Amazon page at Amazon.com/author/jayschulman or JaySchulman.com/book

Blog

This is what started my journey to the book you are reading. I publish posts on Mondays and Wednesdays on growing your information security career. It is definitely the companion to this book. Read the blog at JaySchulman.com.

PODCAST

This book and the podcast are very focused on my thoughts and beliefs. I wanted a medium that would allow for others to talk about their security careers. I created the Building A Life and Career in Security podcast to do just that. It is published in two seasons -- Fall and Spring. You can find the podcast on iTunes or at JaySchulman.com/podcast.

EMAIL

If all else fails, shoot me an e-mail at book@jayschulman.com. I am happy to interact with readers. Send me your comments, questions, or suggestions.

ABOUT THE AUTHOR

Building a Life and
Career in Security

JAYSCHULMAN.COM

JAY SCHULMAN has spent the last 18 years in information security working with some of the biggest organizations in the world. He lives in Chicago with his family. Jay loves educating and inspiring other security professionals to grow their information security careers.

Learn more about Jay at JaySchulman.com

OTHER BOOKS BY JAY SCHULMAN

Currently in process in the series:

- CISO Handbook
- How to Hire a CISO

ONE LAST THING...

If you enjoyed this book or found it useful I would be very grateful if you would post a short review on Amazon. Your support really does make a difference and I read all the reviews personally so I can get your feedback and make this book even better.

If you would like to leave a review then all you need to do is click the review link on this book's page on Amazon here: http://amzn.to/1TGKhnG.

Thanks again for your support!

Printed in Great Britain
by Amazon